Books by Jack Grapes

A Savage Peace
Seven Is A Frozen Number
Two Poets (with Shael Herman)
Perchance, In All Your Travels,
          Have You Ever Been To Pittburgh?
Anything Is A Conversation
Termination Journal
Breaking On Camera
AfterImage (Kita Shantiris)
Presto! (with Vern Maxam)
Some Life

Trees, Coffee,
and the
Eyes of Deer

Trees
Coffee
And The
Eyes of Deer

Jack Grapes

Bombshelter Press

Los Angeles, 1995

Library of Congress Catalog Number: 86-72642

ISBN 0-941017-20-6

PRINTED IN THE UNITED STATES OF AMERICA

ACKNOWLEDGEMENTS

Some of the poems in this book first appeared in the following publications: *AfterImage, Alcatraz, The Alley Cat Readings, Angel's Gate Review, As Each Unit Is A Constant, Bachy, Bellingham Review, Beverly Hills Playhouse Newsletter, Beyond Baroque MAGAZINE, Black Rabbit Press, Blue Window, California State Quarterly, Chattahoochee Review, Comic Spirit, CQ-Contemporary Quarterly, Cream City Review, Deepest Valley Review, Electrum, The Fantastic, Foreign Exchange, Gorilla Extract, Gypsy, Labris, L.A. Weekly, Momentum, Lingo, My Eyes All Out Of Breath, New Lantern Club Review, Nexus, Ole, Orange County Poetry Anthology, Pinchpenny, Poetry/LA, Poetry Magazine, rara avis, Rufus, Scree, Shattersheet, Spillway, Stone Cloud, Sycamore Review, This Poem Knows You, Up:jut, Vagabond, Voices, Vol No, Waves, Wormwood Review, Yellow Fingers*; and the following anthologies: *Gridlock, The Maverick Poets, Men of Our Time, News From Inside, Nueva Poesia de Los Angeles, Poetry Loves Poetry,* and *Stand Up Poetry.*

Many of these poems were written while on a Fellowship from the National Endowment for the Arts, whose support is gratefully acknowledged. The author also wishes to thank the California Arts Council for its Artist-in-Residence grants during the last several years.

Cover photo of the author by Samuel Grapes.

Bombshelter Press
P.O. Box 481270
Bicentennial Station
Los Angeles, CA 90048

For Lori
who got me here

and for Joshua
who keeps us going

CONTENTS

What counted was mythology of self,
.... until nothing of himself
Remained, except some starker, barer self
In a starker, barer world....

He came. The poetic hero without palms
Or jugglery, without regalia.

It purified. It made him see how much
Of what he saw he never saw at all.
He gripped more closely the essential prose
As being, in a world so falsified,
The one integrity for him, the one
Discovery still possible to make,
To which all poems were incident, unless
That prose should wear the poem's guise at last.

Wallace Stevens
"The Comedian As The Letter C"

All The Way Back

All the way back, all the way back and start over,
start over, go all the way back and do it again,
over there, by the tree, go over there, stand over there,
by the tree, walk on over, go all the way over, by the tree,
not by the rock, over by the tree, all the way back,
past the rock, go past the rock, go all the way over and
start again, from the tree, slower, start again slower this
time all the way over past the rock and do it again, without
flinching this time, slowly and without flinching, get your
hands out of your pockets and do it barefoot this time, without
flinching, from the beginning, from the start, from the very
beginning, all the way back without flinching past the rock
slowly and barefoot by the tree and get your hands out of
your pockets, drop the knife, drop the coins, drop the string,
leave them by the tree with your shoes, with your fingernails,
in the box that holds the fire without flinching, that burns
so slowly the flames seem frozen, glittering like swords in
light, without a trace of blood, ice, so dry your skin sticks
to it and comes off, without flinching, from the beginning,
all the way back from the start, go all the way back, and slowly,
as slowly as possible, so slowly you appear to remain still like
that without ever beginning, as if you hadn't yet begun,
when in fact you had begun from the beginning, all the way back
from the start, all the way back, all the way, without flinching.

The Picture

I am five
but that's
not me
in the picture
that's some
one else
who looks
like me
but isn't
me I'm be
hind him
telling
him what
to do with
his mouth
so he'll
look like
me to some
one who does
not know me
if you know
me you know
I look com
pletely diff
rent with
my mouth
shut tight
and my eyes
wide open
and both hands
covering up
my ears so I
won't hear a
thing or say

what I see
when I see
so much
and I'm five,
not even that
yet not until
September
eleventh then
I'll be five.
Imagine when
I'm ten

I Am The Darkness

I am the darkness
Within you all.
I will get you.
Cheat not, tell no man
Lies.
Love those you can
And reserve the others
For boredom
But not pity
And not hatred.
Do not cover your face.
It only becomes
What you are.
Give children pennies
Especially in the winter
Or a candy bar.
Don't cop a feel on a bus
Of a woman
And whatever you do
Don't forget to feed me.
I am the Darkness
Within you all.
I will get you.

Midnight In The Kitchen

The stiff finger of wind—
no, it doesn't come here anymore.
We used to have eggs stacked in the ice box,
two seltzer bottles,
my father's favorite salami and cheese
to snack on after midnight,
when you were you.
You could see
how the mustard spread on the hard bread
by the light of the refrigerator,
the closing door that put the light back in
to keep it cold and stiff
where all the light you need at midnight is
in the ice-box
and you are you
and your mouth tastes the food,
elbows on a porcelain table top,
fat sad eyes in the dead of night
chomp chomp   tick tock
light dark
and you think and you think.
The mouse under the floorboards
breaks a leaf and is gone
knocking a mud-caked coke bottle
against a piece of slate,
and you think and you think
chomp chomp
tick tock
and you are you
getting fat and getting full,
my old lost father
sitting in that midnight kitchen,
1946,
a slow sweep of the hand

and the salt is off the table,
this white rain
spreading on the floor.

Greenhouse Effect

If there is a sound, it is not crying.
To tell you the truth, no noise
comes from the house across the street
where rain collects in the bird bath
on the front lawn, though no bird
ever drinks from it there's so much scum
and floating objects thrown there
by kids walking to and from school.
But where are the children?
We haven't seen any in years,
and the school's been closed,
boarded up, as a matter of fact, burned down,
razed to make a harness factory that shut down
after the strike and sits in disrepair.
That's right, it's not a school at all.
But I take the quiet as a blessing.
What's vanished into the asphalt's
best left where it belongs.
No one around here wants any kind of new life.
I lose a shoe, I wear another that doesn't match.
What's the difference. I see a flower,
I snap it off just like that.
Down the street, Eloise invites the weeds in for tea.
The old bushes rake and rummage across the front yard
like the crippled monster from one of the tales
we used to tell the children with a wink. No one winks now.
We are the thing told and like it. Last year a young decorator
working the neighborhood with his red leather briefcase
and white shoes made the mistake of knocking
on one too many doors. We did everything but
eat his bones. Threw them in the bird bath
to rot and stink up the place so they'd never be noticed.
The sun's our only enemy. But we can wait.
Let it come just a little closer.

What The Leaves Make
That Turn In Autumn

What the leaves make that turn in autumn
is pinched from the wind.
On the front porch of my uncle's house
we watched the pony named Pinto
ride down the neutral ground
up and down Elysian Fields Avenue.
What the water tower painted green was green for,
high on its legs, a fresh god,
and I was that child that water
has not come to again.
The hurricane's coming, Aunt Bea said.
Moaning of the dead surrounded the house.
What the windows exed with masking tape faced;
that rags were wrapped for the freeze;
Uncle Charles gone to the store for flashlight batteries;
and the horse called to me,
he was my horse wasn't he.
What the Indians rode when I wished I was with them
to have bare legs against a blanket
and threaten the hills that turn black
when the sun goes behind them.
How did it work: I wondered,
and waited for the work to begin:
The lightning froze our faces first,
then thunder inside steel boots pranced on the roof,
and the rain filled the water tank
where Pinto could drink the next day
after we rode him in the air of a fall afternoon,
where Elysian Fields and Esplanade Avenue meet,
where I want to go again,
to feel that pony's teeth on my hand,
to climb the ladder to the top of the tower
and pick splinters from a green god's hand.

Mardi Gras, 1950

Dressed in a Superman costume,
I fly over them.
Karl is Daniel Boone.
Louis is Davy Crockett.
Charlaine is the baby in the gypsy outfit.
I fly over them.
Beer in the streets.
Is it a man or a woman
my mother asks
as it swishes by and flips up
showing crinoline
and a bare ass.
I fly over him.
King Zulu goes by, throw me a coconut
we scream, running after the floats.
Beer in the streets beer cans.
Flambeaux carriers dressed in white robes, struttin'
where ya' at, mutha!
Harem girls, spacemen, monkeys
in monkey suits.
I fly over them.
Sick in the streets, wine in the streets.
The floats go by throw me something mister!
Music the bands drunks singing.
I fly over them.
The Indian princess kisses Dracula.
Don't step in the vomit! my mother yells.
Frankenstein's holding a glass from Pat O'Brien's
filled with pink punch and rum;
he sips from a long pink straw.
The Devil with his pitchfork gooses Buck Rodgers.
Broken glass and confetti float down the gutter.
Someone steps on the pink hot dog bun.
Dad sneaks a drink as he hugs

the lady in the cowboy suit.
Raiders from Mars!
Black leather jackets and boots!
Flowers out of the magician's mouth!
I fly over them.
Gangs with razor blades snug in the tips of their shoes.
Faces with knives.
Police shoving the crowd back.
Drunks singing in the beer streets.
Pissing in the streets.
Knives in the streets.
Faces in the streets.
Throw me something, mister!
Throw me something, mister!
Throw me something.

Boom goes the drum.

What Drove Damon Down

a short thunder is what drove Damon down,
and not meant to be confused, he stood on the corner
of Pico and Alvarado until the rain was in his pocket
next to the bumble-bee (how he loved anything that bumbled,
Damon was that kind of a guy)
and cried himself to sleep.
His mother came by once,
and in Africa he saw himself a huge rhino
(when are rhinos small, I know)
snorting in a pool of water.
Once in Woolworth's Damon took a toy airplane
trembling it under his coat
and all the way home on a bus
even under his pillow trembling
then finally down in the dark corner of his closet
where it stayed until he was past his third wife,
the plane was gone,
Damon never knew who took it.
"I want meat!" he shouted, pounding his chest
with one clenched fist holding a fork.
Damon liked pigeons.
Damon fixed flat tires.
Damon was in love with women.
Damon kept looking for things that would change his life.
A book, a poem, a stranger on the streetcar.
The end came in July.
Damon was in bed, smelling the hot okra sidewalk
and listening to the rain.
This is old, he thought, looking at his skin,
but if I was never young
why do I remember my pet turtle, hollow in the sun;
the hard washcloth my mother rouged against my cheeks;
no one's moon but my own
outside the window next to my crib?

Then thunder came in, and
Damon said it was too short,
and he went down.

Someone In The Next Room
Goes Mad, 1953

Aunt Adela is pushing fish into the grinder.
Aunt Fanny swings around the dining room
talking and bumping her ass
into the table set for Passover.
On diet pills, she's a 45 year old speed freak.
My mother sits in the kitchen
on her fat hams, fat thighs, fat arms,
cheeks in a bulge
like a moored battleship unfit for tourists.
Bernice in white maid's uniform
understands the Yiddish passed
between these women, why not,
she was there when my grandmother
shriveled in her wheelchair, yelling in Yiddish,
"Too much noise, the children
make too much noise."
We ran around her wheelchair whooping like Indians.

This is the exhibit at the World's Fair
next to the Disney version of frontier life:
Mrs. Boone does the wash out back:
Abe Lincoln's father drags home a deer.

In the next panel is the home of the future.
There's me and my family wearing red jump suits,
staring out the windows—magic panes
that do not break and keep out the cold,
where nothing freezes or burns or rusts or goes crazy,
and you're forbidden to remember the past.

In the next panel
strapped to a chair,
someone is writing this down.

Nothing Left To Chance

Begin with fish,
smack their heads off with a mallet
or tear through the entire phone book
sheet by sheet
and digest the lives listed
five hundred to a page.
You don't remember one old phone number
but all the addresses
for each home you've lived in
bob like little boats
on the ocean of your daydreams.
You can't understand why poets
write lines like that,
or what makes a car go,
and when you see those steel girders
going up on the vacant lot,
the exposed elevatorshafts,
glass and concrete not far behind
you wonder how so much can be built
one piece at a time
and nothing left to chance.

Arms That Take You In

She does not climb
the star of lion,
had nettles put in place
and takes your face
home in a bag.
Now she was clever, all right.
Each night she removes
her robe, butchered
ankles with one swoop
and the flapping trips
the alarm swarming
the place with cops.
This is it.
The face tucked safely
into her pocket,
she fades back and fades
to this day,
whether full-mooned
or in charge,
each arm takes you in,
without phony,
without pensions or blue playthings,
without kisses or kissing,
trumpets or slander,
without one sign or sure word,
a warning hiss—nothing.
I mean nothing at all.
She stands there
in clever home and opens her robe
flaps naked arms
and takes you in and to this day
she takes you in.
. . . .

She returns the turtle

with both legs open,
strokes the inside of her thighs
on a tie,
each knot passing
port cities and storms
above the oceans.
This is the wrong place,
but she waves the curtains back.
and shoves me down by the one light
on the bedstand,
uncertain headlights that circle
these walls in my sleep.
Crunch for one tabletop;
a breath that is good as gold.
By now, I am sweating.
I can slide off the muscles
of her skin.
Trombones.
Glaring spoons of bugles
where the flesh snarls glue,
butler, pussy, reingold,
shifting asses surfing on the bedspread,
fluctuate,
blaze down and into her,
she tuggles me in and bugles me out,
both legs open,
each knot passing,
she strokes the poor cities
on the inside of her thighs
and returns the turtle,
a breath that is good as gold.
......

Who are we? Not Noble.
We confuse structure with bear-traps
and bears for a song.
But there is no music,

just her humming by the dresser
as she returns each part of her panties
to her legs,
not a clasp notwithstanding.

The rhyme is with the lion.
A picture hanging crooked on the wall;
a window shade unsprung;
the mirror on the closed closet door.
And the radio on.
I am only back where the old entrance
remains open.
the rest in hand.
A glacier that humbles Tuesdays
in my mouth and raises welts
if I suck too hard.
There is no sign.
There is only this turning,
this constant turning.
She adds a blouse,
a skirt,
a pair of high-heeled shoes
and hums,
what is the tune?
The tune is not the mirror
but one belt loop missed
is all I'd need to find her;
just this nickel in the palm of my hand.
Then she raises her arms like a dancer,
takes a deep golden breath of bars,
and goes.

Lizards, Backs, and
Shoes As They Are

Someone's overturned the lake again.

I do not understand this one word here, he says.
Neither do I, which is why I keep it in.
But countless things escape so easily out of you,
he gasps.
Are you gasping? Actually gasping?
He apologizes, says he's been reading too much.

And someone's given birth to a brilliant lizard.
Perhaps you know the mother. Clues abound.
Geography is so bare: Like a wet fish
the thumbprint on the refrigerator
wiggles across the chrome.
You'll have to explain that one, he says.
But we meet each other in so many different places,
I yell (yelling is allowed).
First you march up to the door and swing it open.
Then you learn the beast's language, full of eager notes
and Yippee! the soldiers are home!
Who minds their muddy boots.
Look at the moon how full it is.
My what a moon you say and see,
our problems are gone already.
Meet you at midnight with the fox of the evil evening,
backslapping summer mouth full of sucking flowers.

Ah, but a hundred miles away the city is being eaten.

Who's in charge of burning all these papers? someone asks.
Now this incessant questioning will just have to stop.
We'll never get anything done this way.
Count the bodies again. Are any new? Keep just a few.

And Monday, the notary publics. The sheets
and the suits with no names attached,
false teeth still in their cup
and Wednesday too, missing with the rest
no one puts anything away, sheets of dead skin
hard and brittle crunching underfoot
static on the radio, fire drills, children
in the street hitting other children
with long cracking sticks.
Who is going to marry at a time like this?

There is so much and so much to do.
Let us be vegetables together or bubble gum.
Let's make love while the broccoli cooks.
Let's mail our shoes to the richest men on earth.
Who can ask questions with so much to be done?
And so many shoes piled by the door as we sleep.

Which Cup, Which Eye

The cup has come to his hand
and she says
which eyes
which eyes were you talking about.
He has begun to remove
her hands
which float up without complaint
each finger spread
apart
as if to say
no more.
A look out the window
reveals
the possibilities:
first the long black automobile
stranded with rust and bullets;
then the rubber knife beside
a leo lion puppet
and over by the trunk of the tree
crackling through the sidewalk
the book, stiff against the wind,
still wet,
covered with muddy footprints.

Which eyes,
she says again.
The eyes that approximate,
he says,
that remove tissue
without cutting bone;
eyes that
like your hands,
spread apart
as if to say

no more.
He opens the door and looks out
but there is no one, nothing.
Someone just a minute ago was listening.
He recognized the face.
They've seen us, she says.
Yes
and the skin
begins to come away
without a sound
from their heads.

And This Is My Father

Up
up
up.
Up through five green
hospital floors I run the
elevator up through five
green hospital floors
to where my father walks
along the clean halls
hands in his red robe
to meet me stepping out
to meet him.
A pale hand on my shoulder,
he takes me deep-dyed in ceremony
to the nurse's station
where all the work to be done
is flourished in rich flames
and slow thighs
that squeeze through the night shift.
"This is my son," he says
but I catch the stare of the red-headed
nurse turning her blood-dimmed face to mine.
It is the night shift;
she is the shadow of an indignant falcon.
My father spreads his thick pale hand
with me within it
down the halls into each living room
not staked with hanging vines
of water and blood.
"This is my son," he says to Mr. William
thickening in his heart.
"This is my son," he says to Mr. Butler
covered to the neck with a sheet.
"This is my son," he says

to whomever we pass in the hall.
The dying glide without glee
in their beds;
birds fly at the windows
and turn back.
"When are you coming home?" I ask.
My father smiles and his hand opens wide
without fear floating up to his ear, scratching.
The tall nurse catches him out of bed.
"What are you doing out of bed!" she thunders.
"Why, this is my son," he says to her
carrying off in astonishment
the fully mortal laugh of all his teeth.
And this is my father,
long after his death has died
haunting the night shift hospitals
with the relish
of a gypsy.

How Simple A Poem Is

it means to see to see the pitiful
handful of ashes you hold
as you move toward the horizon
singing and making a monument
on a road no one will pass
ever in your life time it means
to run against the wind mouth open
like a nut escaped from adjacent
territories of the interior the radiant
bedfellow of foolishness it means
to believe to believe that you
can be this far from the center
of the earth and still feel the fire
that washes up from the core it means
to stop to stop at once give birth
to whatever is handy that does
as it will do for no one
but yourself
for now

American River

A few birds
go into the fresh sky.

Someone sings gaily
along the black river.

It sure is a pleasure
California.

Look down upon the fork
of the American River.

Lie there in the sun;
a brown and fired look.

God, is that a peach?
Juicy as a watermelon.

Last night at sunset
I pointed out the pink sky.

This is the place to live.
Even at night, it's bright as day.

Pretend

Pretend you don't see me
behind the typewriter.
Pretend the words
were always just this way
on the page
before the face
of the one
who wrote them
in his underwear
on a cold November 5 a.m. Monday
morning
thinking about the commercial audition
he has today at 3:15
for Benson & Hedges.
Thinking should I shave
my mustache,
should I cut my hair,
should I wear a suit,
should I tap dance?
Thinking my sister lives
two thousand miles away
and at 20
hasn't what it takes
to live the next 30.
Thinking why was my wife crying
over the toilet when I walked
into the bathroom.
Pretend I have no face,
no name, no history.
Pretend
the poem's
the thing
that dies.

Holding On

It's been such a long time holding on.
I die with the ones I love
and they go on without me.
Is that me in the photograph?
Jack, do you see me looking at you?
Do you know that camera is the future,
and there is nothing out there
but me, looking back at you,
wondering whether to rip you out
as if you were the imposter.
I have forgotten what you seemed to know,
smiling as you climb out of the pool,
sliding hair out of your eyes,
no rush to get your medal,
just a pause to let your tan body glisten.
What did you know that you could wait
a winner at the lens.
I am tired of your marvel.
I dare you to leave that picture
and walk with me now and remain beautiful.
I'm the one who has marched backwards
to keep you where you are.
I'm the one who holds onto all the family movies & pictures,
boxes and boxes of beanstalk seeds.
My body dies to keep you alive.
My spirit dies in your name.
I'm the one who writes this
unable to hold on.

Feeding Time

The horse
in the house
is not dead
but he pretends to be.

"Get that horse out of the bathroom!"
my wife screams.

The crows beat on the doors.
"We want our money!" they cry.
My five buck friends I call them.

I am in the attic—
the giraffe—
sticking my head out the window.
"No one's home," I shout down.

And you know what's in the belfry.
My wife complains.
"Move out," I say, "if you don't like it."

She moves out, taking
Morgan the canary,
Trigger the cat,
Bruce the dog,
and Lassie,
our pet hamster.

So it's the horse and me.
One of us pretending to be dead.
The other, stretching his neck out in a dry season,
reading leaves,
cleaning ash trays on the coffee table,
cooking up a roast in the kitchen.

The tigers are coming for dinner.

Listen

Listen, what are you reading this for?
Haven't you got bills to pay,
a movie you've been wanting to see,
a woman to love or a wife to ignore.
I'm here because it's raining,
and poets write poems when it rains—
at least that's what I read once somewhere.
(Listen, I'm lying to you. It's not raining.
I just said that because it sounded good.
It's a beautiful day. There's liable to be a law
or a proverb dealing it a blow from which
it may never recover that's how beautiful a day
it is and you should find a girl or a football
and a field of clover
to take them both
around around around.)

Are you reading this to feel better?
Do you think writing this makes me feel better?
Let me tell you something.
You know what'll make me feel better?
A million dollars. A million million dollars.
I want to be corrupted by money and fame
so bad it squeaks my socks.
I want to be filthy with money
to buy filthy men out
and sell their souls
for a bucket of paint.
I want to have so much money
I'll be able to rob my own bank,
buy my way *in* and *out* of jail,
cook omelettes from golden goose's eggs,
send every starving poet
a twenty dollar cook book

and laugh in their faces
saying:

I don't need your words!
I don't need your poems!
I don't need your books or your dreams.
I don't need your aches and pains
and sensational sufferings!
I don't need your visions
your eyes your goddamn poet's eyes!
I've Got Money, Baby!
I'VE GOT ALL THE MONEY
IN THE WORLD!
I OWN THE EARTH AND THE SUN
AND THE PLANETS
AND THE STARS I DON'T OWN,
NO ONE CAN BUY!
I CAN BE GOD! I CAN BE GOD!

. . . .

Listen, I didn't mean what I wrote.
I got a little carried away.
You'll forgive me because it's raining.
I get carried away when it rains.
I don't want money.
I don't want power.
I don't want to own men's souls.
I want just to be poet.
To write words of startling beauty
to fill the universe
of emptiness
in your soul.
To make the trees dance
and the winds curl back upon themselves
like confetti off a ship.

I want your tears.
I want to reach
the depth of such beauty—
I want the universe to suffer
because beauty is a pain beyond pain
that dies in the willow
as well as in the wars of men.
I want all men to own my soul,
the poet's soul,
for it's always for the asking.
I want to belong to all the nations,
and all the oceans.
I want to belong to the earth,
the planets,
all the stars,
and all the spaces
beyond all spaces.
I want to be god.

How The Stranger Is

How is the stranger.
He's okay.
See him eating in the kitchen.
Dirty boots full of mud.
But he likes the ham sandwich.

How he got in
I don't know.
It was so early when he knocked.
Go take a peek.
Is he still eating?

Now the mailman comes for a coke
and the two of them chat.
Perhaps they know each other.
I walk around the house
thinking what to do.
The stranger comes out and
asks me what I want.
What *I* want? I say.
But he laughs and punches my arm,
then sits in front of the TV
and watches.
Should I talk to him?
Three paintings by van Gogh
on the wall I got at Sears
he likes, says they remind him of home.
Are they still fixing the street? he asks.
I go out and look, but nothing's there.
He laughs when I come back.
Tricked again, and he punches me on the arm.
He punches me again, harder.
Then again, harder, and again
on the other arm, with his other hand.

What's for dinner, he asks.
He asks to see my maps, all my maps:
The close-up of the Salton Sea
and Lake Pontchartrain.
He punches me again, harder.
Hey, I yell, that was pretty hard.
He smiles, takes the salami and cuts it in half
with the large bread knife.
Want to cut, he asks,
all big teeth showing in his smile
and he hands me the knife.
Go ahead, he says. Cut.
Tonight he throws all the pillows on the floor,
takes the chairs and sets them
against the walls.
He stomps around the house
with those big boots and leaves mud tracks
in the kitchen and on the carpet on the stairs.
He goes about dumping everything on the floor,
sweeping his hand around the cabinets and cupboards.
Bam-bam, he one-twos me in the stomach
with each fist,
then *slap-slap* in the face.
Big meaty hands.
Slap-slap again.
Chairs through the windows.
Kicks in the TV.
Books topple from the shelves.
Hurls the telephone into the bathtub
that is already filled with water
and overflowing.
Have a cigar, he says.
Have a cigar.
The stranger lights it for me,
and watches me puff on it
and lights one for himself,
and gestures me to sit down with him

next to the overturned sofa
and we sit
blowing smoke above our heads.
Real fine, he says, dontcha think?
Yep, I say.
Real fine.

Lights In The Museum

My brother wears long-sleeved shirts
that cover the tracks on his arms.
He lives alone now in the big house;
we've all married and moved out
or died.
Louis stalks the rooms like a walrus
and forgets to turn out
the lights.
I come home for a visit and hear
the ghost of my father complaining
about the light bill.
"Louis, turn out the lights
when you leave a room," I tell him.
As he leaves each room, he remembers
and lurches back,
slamming his arm
on the wall,
hoping to find the light switch;
and this is how I see him
after I've gone:
lurching from one room to another,
lights on,
lights off.
The lights in my home back home
go on and off
day and night
all year long.

My brother could hop fences
like a deer
and my father once took his picture,
a freckled face covered with dirt
and peanut butter and jelly
smeared on his chin;

a photograph that once hung
in the Delgado Museum for a month.
It was titled *The All American Boy*
because the confederate hat he wore
had "The All American Boy"
written across the top band,
but with that face and freckles,
there was no mistake that here,
under the hat,
was the real thing:
the all-American boy.

That photograph hung with others
along walls full of light switches
and someone going from room to room
turning out the lights—
a woman giving tours through the museum.

My home back home is like a museum.
In it my brother is a photograph
that moves down the halls,
meaty hands and shirt tail hanging out,
freckles and tracks on his face and arms.
Everything about that photograph
my brother has become
moves like the flesh
of an old lake.
Everything moves but his eyes.
They stare without direction,
and it is hard to tell
whether behind them
the light
is on
or off.

Another Poem

The simmered center of your life
hardens on a teaspoon.

You do not begin
at the beginning.
You begin at the end
of a brutal whiteness
when the heart has lost its nerve,
the incomprehensible hand
.hat reaches for the incomprehensible razor
waits for the death of the body
that follows the death of the heart
which refuses
in spite of its name
to die,
and if you don't know this already,
it will take more than poetry
to teach you.
After all, life is a tomato,
whatever that means.
It is also a wristwatch, and by and by
a pencil.

In the middle of watching *Beloved Infidel* on TV,
a movie I've seen four times and know by heart,
I come here to do this, to write,
to stir up the soup of my life, as it were.
My wife and I are not living together now.
: wonder how my brother is,
eating up the skin on his arms,
trying to save his life, his tomato,
his wristwatch.
The high point of my day these day.
is getting a peach at Farmer's Market.

These facts are only of my life;
like yours, elegant as they are dull.

But I come here to write this
to save my life, when it is a tomato,
a wristwatch, and by and by a pencil.
So what's to save?
On channel 9 Victor Mature is an Indian;
On channel 13 Matt Dillon kisses the girl
and carries sacks of flour to her house;
On Channel 4 they're dancing to Isaac Hayes.

It's about time I end this poem,
wrap it up like laundry to drop at your feet.
I know you need these loose ends tied up.
When a man sits down to save his
tomato,
as it were,
it's the least he can do.
And the truth of it is, I can do it.
I'm a good enough poet to do it.
I know how to begin and end a poem.
But just now,
on the edge of a pain
I can't point to or name,
I don't feel like it.
My life is not a tomato.
My life is not a wristwatch.
My life is not a by and by.
I'm going to watch *Beloved Infidel* end
the same way it always ends.
My ends will all be different.

And this poem?
I'll end it
in another poem.

Burial

Plucking the light above me
I dream in the darkness
of my black mother
a running splash of rust
whose head grows immense
in my arms.

Dazzled and green-eyed
from the streets
I watch brown stockings
fall to her feet.
Coffee blossoms
amazed at the armpits,
to come home
hung by a thread
the brown carcass of my black mother
who has strangled the tired voice
whose head grows immense
in my arms.

She says your mother means well.
I do not tell her
that she is my mother
brown my black mother
asleep in white calico
who rocks with the voice
whose head grows immense
in my arms.

You are not from my country
she says
but I am brown your black mother
I pass fingers through your hair,
come here
high on the tree
to sit when it rains
overgrown with coffee blossoms
my boy   my boy   my boy
I am brown your black mother
my head
grows immense
in your arms.

The Count's Lament

There are not too many ways
to drink the blood.
Thick and slightly warm
like pureed vichyssoise.
Sometimes I roll it around,
what little there is,
in my cheek between tongue and palate,
just to get a taste again
of what I've forgotten the taste of,
drinking it so much now out of desperation
that perhaps even this sip
is not enough anymore.
Perish that horrible thought!
I go now from neck to neck,
throat to throat,
reeling, scratching with my fingernails,
flapping against invisible mist
that issues from their mouths
as they walk about the streets
in a cold that lies above the ground,
a cold you can wave your arms in
should you need to.
Not the cold darkness I bask in.
A darkness that has a taste,
a dull texture that grinds in my sleep.
It's all the same:
Flamingos!
Daffodils!
To dream of a blazing sun,
just think of it,
to dream of that burning
and be unable to touch it,
suck its fire into my own veins,
down the gullet where it boils

the substance of my flesh—
then to wake, biting at splinters.
It's no life for a Count, believe me.
Were I to drive drunken
down one of your neon streets
what breath test would you give me
when even the flesh turns thin and white
at the end of a century.
A century!
It's like a snap to me.
All I vomit is blood.
That sickness comes out of my throat.
To be drunk again for fear of the waste.
The indignity!
Just to stand at the sideboard
with a scotch and ice in my hand
and clank the cubes around the glass
and finish it off with a puff.
The worms. The rats. The beetles.
The spider spinning its web
for the unwary fly,
tiny cracks of blood I've long disdained.
And now all there is left
is you,
your own meager supply
that brightens with my pulse.
Imagine what it might be like
to flow in my veins
for centuries without end.

Ask The Bulls

What are you sure of?
Ask the bulls.
The kill must be easy,
quick if you can
manage it,
but easy if nothing else.

So you're outside Mexico City.
The local boys torture the bulls.
Their silk is full of sweat and dust.
On wooden benches
you sit watching
and crack pistachios
between your teeth.
You don't see blood
until the black animal
is dragged through the dust
on ropes and chains
like a stalled truck.
The *banderilleros* push
from behind, churning
their thin legs.
Flies buzz lazily
in the plaza.

Now you know
you are going
to write a poem about this.
Down the aisles the kids
had yelled all afternoon:
"Piece da cheese! Piece da cheese!"
waving little bags in the air.
Why are they selling
pieces of cheese, you thought,

but finally buy,
and as the bull
is being dragged through the dirt
you crack the "piece da cheese"
between your teeth,
spitting shells into the ring.

You look around,
at the fat *afficionado*
displeased with the slow kill.
The bull's neck hanging
to the ground.
The matador stands over him,
hands above his head
like a dancer in fifth position
to drive the blade in.
He thrusts six, seven times
and the bull is weary
and no one watches.

You see this all
taking place
not just now,
but later,
in the poem,
in the poem you will write:
the flags and the ceremony
and the fat *picadores*
grunting in the saddles
of their horses;
the hot sun, the animal smell,
fierce ladies in yellow hats
shaking their fists for blood.

You sit back, smug and grateful,
the empty page of the poem
folded in your back pocket.

You know just how it will go.
There's no need to rush it.
Anytime you need it,
the poem's yours.

An easy kill.

Suspect

Suspect
the poem
that is not
a matter
of life & death.
It is like
all the other
poems
that are not
matters
of life & death.
When a man
talks to you
without
blinking an eye,
when a man
listens
without glancing
over his shoulder,
his hand
is on a knife
and he knows
what he wants.
He wants
your crippled mother
clutching that
foolish poem
in her
wheelchair
hands.

I was much further out than you thought
And not waving but drowning.

Stevie Smith

Invisible

Dispatch: blue baby left
   in back seat
   outmaneuvers rat
for rattle.

Sun goes down. Sun comes up.
   No one touches me.
Even in plain sight: hiding.

They come to my room.
These are his things:
   a dozen pipes;
   five thousand books;
   pennies by the jarful.

Just what is too much to ask
   when you're invisible:
that they leave you alone?

She Fucks And I Fuck

She fucks and I fuck
and both of us are fucking
Now I'm up, I'm thinking I'm fucking
then I'm not thinking I'm fucking
I'm just fucking
Then I'm telling her how good it feels
then I'm feeling how good it feels
I want to come and I don't want to come
She wants to come and she doesn't
want to come, oh not just yet
you can't fuck and think about fucking
all at the same time, your leg is in
her cunt all of a sudden and you want
to be her cunt all of a sudden
to be fucked, not to fuck,
to include, not to penetrate,
to be killed, not the killer
Oh and it's always moving,
it's going to be over
suddenly you think and then you don't think,
A tongue licks your closed eye
and it licks your closed chest
and you lick back,
thinking of licking,
then just licking
and your heart breaks,
it breaks,
you're fucking the woman you love
and it breaks your heart.
You're deep and full
in pity and in pain,
coming up from life
for air,

and yes, I love me now,
I am plunged and raised,
set down and risen,
the inside breaks against the bone,
and God, dear God,
if You could fuck the woman You love
when You are loving her,
everything that hurts
in Your heart
would come true.

State Of The Union

Me, Tarzan; You Jane.
This is how physics
gets at the nature of things.
Once I thought I'd see everything.
Then be able to show it.
Like I could love you,
and solve everything.
A philosopher told me
not to use the word *thing*,
that it was vague,
meaning among other things,
affair, event, deed, act,
possession, accomplishment,
circumstance, detail,
individual, and especially,
person.
Sleep is a stabbed animal.
Life is out there.
I am in here.

Recitative

When the bottoms of tables re-embrace their
former students and the doorbells embark
upon stranger journeys inward,
keep this edge in your face that you know
which friend to love and lover to betray.

If there are words to be said to those
who threaten with their kneecaps
better to move against the wall sideways
like an animal in the zoo who keeps secret
which friend to love and lover to betray.

Certainly it's no use being skillful;
show your naked body to the camera even
when the background's similar; those
who look look back and fail to answer
which friend to love and lover to betray.

If you cannot sleep, sleep will pay no debts;
if your hands are shamed into motionlessness
take care that your feet scrape
the proper mud from your shoes and lead you to
which friend to love and lover to betray.

I've got no answers. A coat or sweater
works as well as a shelf though a bed
unobserved is no place to dream or cut your
wrists. Cut your eyeballs out if they know
which friend to love and lover to betray.

Never mind. This is taller than you are.
A movement to the window. Out there the name,
walking on its fingertips, at the edge
of the face, on the tongue of each friend
who loves you and each lover you betray.

The Beast And The Dreamer

There is a beast
in the bed with you.
You'd rather pretend
it's the dream
or the overcoat
you forgot to hang up
or that person
you share space with
on the sheets.
When you roll into him
during the night
and his teeth fly up
to the ceiling,
you hold still,
listen for a sound
to explain it,
look for the book
you fell asleep reading,
then roll back over,
and the beast settles
down again beside you
like a black balloon.

I know about this beast.
He does not sleep
and he does not dream.
To himself, if asked,
he is more a beast,
knows his ugliness
to become more ugly.
Swamps dry up in his mouth.
The death of ships
under the ocean

slide in slime on his skin.
His arms are the broken
bones of asteroids,
his eyes
the open ass of Krakatoa.

And though he's never died,
his death is all he truly remembers.
Condemned to the light within the dark of sleep,
he is not permitted his own,
but puts one arm
behind his head
and thinks through the night
with you,
avoiding the beast of thoughts.
He lies beside you,
envious of your slow breathing,
wishing your dreams
were his to dream,
wanting just one
of your nightmares
to wake from.

This Storm, And The Next One

All of this pain
is an envelope.
Look what upsets you:
a spilled glass
of apple juice
and your kids
why worry about them?
Where are your parents now,
now that you tie your shoes
and ignore your wife
who locks the doors
when you go.
An envelope, a chair,
a dish of almonds,
that ridiculous $40
hand-painted
waste-paper basket.
Today the city is under mud.
The sun comes out
and everyone's back
to buying hamburgers and gum.
I'll bet your suit is pressed.
My shoes are wet
and still I wear them
but no big thing.
Was that a neighbor of yours
who carried a bag of valuables
into the den
just before the water
swept his bedroom down the hill?
An envelope.
A chair.
A plate of cheese.

Did you read about the winter Olympics
with transit strikes and Soviet medals?
This Lake Placid is that what you mean
by pain?
An envelope.
A chair.
A line of tanks and bombs.
And what of that Greek
who burned the enemy's fleet down
by reflecting sunlight off the shields
of his men.
And that shoemaker in the lava of Pompei,
still bent over his workbench.
Envelopes, chairs, shoes, shields.
The sky is getting dark again.
They say the next storm is 200 miles
off the coast, due later tonight.
Well, it's me reaching up and dragging
all that rain down.
That's my hand going up black
behind the bushes.
Remember this storm years from now
when you are swept into the cities
by the cities,
and into the sea by the sea.
This one: an envelope,
a chair,
a line of hands
reading your own hands' future.
Stay in tonight.
Lock the doors.

Strange Visitors

I believe I have seen
whole houses lift right up
and fly off, without
a sound.

Now, the doorbell rings
and I pull my pants
up my walking legs
to get there
before my miracle goes away.

But it's just two tall girls
of the Jehovah Witness—
clean and fresh flesh
under thin summer dresses
and they put into my hands
lit-te r-a-tchure, instead of their own hands.

"Look," I say, "I'm an atheist,
thank you anyway."
But they keep their smiles
and come right back.
"An atheist! Well, we can fix that.
See here on page ten
where the light
came out of the sky
and the face of the void was full?"
And I listen to their talk
full of bloom and bubbles,
shaking my head, "Ahuh, ahuh..."
Then finally:
"Look, I was beating off
when you rang the bell.

Could you come back in about ten minutes.
I'm almost finished."

I believe I have seen
strange visitors from other planets
unwrap salami sandwiches
in the park, plastic forks
in cups of chopped liver.
I believe I have seen strange faces
disappear in supermarkets.

My sister called today, long distance,
to tell me my brother's
shooting up again.
"We haven't seen him in weeks, Jack
and I'm scared."
"Charlaine," I say, "maybe he just
went to visit that girl in Houston.
Maybe he just had to get away,
fly off somewhere."
"Maybe," she says.

The light in the sky goes away
and the night comes now
in one large, slow footstep.
I have been feeling ancient lately.
Something in me wants to go back.

I look out the window.
There goes another house.
In the distance, it looks
as it rises
like a kite.
And the doorbell rings.
And the phone rings.
And my hands,
blooming with fingers,

ring,
waiting to be answered.
And my hands, strange visitors,
fly off,
and take me
with them.

Copernicus

The whale at the extremity of the nose
the most eastern of the three in the jaw,
begins to the south at the first bend in the water
greater than fourth magnitude
and brings it to the mouth of the southern fish.

To the west and on the dark
at the head of the arrow
the more obscure on the left shoulder
the goat remains three in the middle of the body
the brighter of the two
and heel.

The dragon
in the tongue
on the jaw
above the eye
in the cheek
above the head
the most northern in the first curve of the neck
and the unconstellated between the thighs
which they call Arcturus

On the head
on the breast
on the girdle
above the seat, at the hips
at the knees
on the leg
at the extremity of the foot

at the mouth
on the head

in the middle of the neck
in the breast
the most brilliant in the tail
in the elbow of the right wing
in the flat on the wing
the middle one
the more western of the two

the greater   the smaller   the obscure

the star which is the first of all and the more
of the two on the horn
the bright one at the extremity of the river
in the hollow of the right foot

neither at rest nor in the center
at the point that makes the center,
unmoving.

Break Down

Of course, you're alone.
In America, on a Texas highway
watching the last smoke of the sun
grow black.
Without oil, without gas,
without a pay phone that works.
Tonight, you'll be killed:
that, you know.
A drunk pick-up does it as a joke,
or the night swans
who prowl for your kind,
who leave your shoes,
and take the camera,
the luggage, the money.
You're alone, you're going
to be dead, if you walk
toward the closed Texaco station
one mile up or sit it out till morning,
you're going to be dead.
Where were you going? El Paso?
On the map, for some reason,
you circled Carlsbad and Sonora.
The last for gas, you thought.
Then:
A pair of tail-lights turn
on the gravel shoulder
and slowly become headlights.
You begin to laugh,
make an outstretched gesture
with both arms wide
as if sending aloft
a dazed insect
from the palm
of each hand.

The Long Poem

The long poem
has brought seven friends
to help carry in
all his luggage

Buzzard

Buzzard makes the mountain
and says to me:
"The light. I made the light, too
and cracked those rays in my throat,
tasted what you call flesh
but was plaster, then copper,
then rusted pipe,
the blade of a knife still sharp.
Is this what your people
have come to?"

The snows melt and take with them
the cave raging of the buffalo.
My first dance. Will she dance
with me? If I squeeze her hand
will she squeeze back, and if that,
then what?
Buzzard flaps in my chest.
He wants out.
He wants to follow the trains
but to meet no train
that stops.
He wants to trust the trees
and melt the cities down
to mercury and sulphur.
Buzzard says:
"I can eat my own kind, too.
It wasn't easy, but you taught me.
And I make the light;
I go up and lay the killing
at the feet of the father
and bless its food.
Reason will justify anything

but bless the poetry
and the light will bring you up."

He has a point.
Some days, we sit in the yard
and listen to the rain
shatter on the tin shed
by the plum tree
or watch it from the bedroom window
clog the backyard drain.

Buzzard shuts his eyes and takes
my hand.

"You have two homes," he says,
"but you can only die
in one."

My Rodeo

I'm ashamed of my cheap rodeo
so I keep it secret from my friends.
It's not even as big as theirs
and needs constant repair.
"How's your rodeo?" someone asks at a party.
"Fine!" they chirp up.
They jump at the chance
to extol the virtues of their rodeo.
Pretty soon a circle gathers
and everyone's discussing its size,
weather control, the acoustics, the peanuts.
If I stay in my corner someone will notice and ask about mine.
I don't want to talk about it.
So I join in, chirping up with *you-don't-says*,
and *isn't-that-amazings* and
what-about-the-functional-glitter?

By the time I get home
I'm exhausted from avoiding the subject of my rodeo.
I get home and there it is,
not much on weather control, lousy acoustics,
styrofoam peanuts.
There's no sub-culture, no glitz-trimming,
no contour illuminations, not even jacket hitch
where the top bolt exceeds the maintenance quota lining.
I'm embarrassed and ashamed of the damn thing,
give it a kick and stub my toe, then cover it with a sheet.
Maybe smother it.

I am a man who comes home depressed, lonely,
frustrated, who tries to smother his rodeo,
his cheap rodeo.
And I haven't even the courage to do that.

Imagine smothering one's rodeo.
The shame would haunt me the rest of my life.
So after awhile I take the sheet off and go to bed,
hear its slight breathing throughout the night,
its occasional cough, the short low moan
just before daybreak. My cheap rodeo.

The Easy Part

The Eiffel Tower's on the cover,
cubist, prismatic, unshaven.
I watch the rain
shine up the earth, layer by layer.
Je vois tomber la pluie.
It's all one kind of rain
or another:
rain in the teeth,
rain in the palm of the hand.
It stops everyone from talking,
this yet and yet.
Once around the earth.
There is someone
who wishes to sleep beside you,
and you consent.
Because this is the easy part.
Just before sleep.
Just what your life has been
up to now:
a bird, a little bird;
so many things,
on their way to postage.

Butcher

Butcher sipping tea.
Butcher fishing with the cord tied round his neck
    as he leans over the bank, thinking:
    trout or shark.

Butcher notices his mother's getting old.
    Cradles her wrinkled arm in his hand.
    Takes a peek at the other arm in the
    bottom drawer beside the bed.

Butcher's asleep now, so don't disturb him.
    Tip-toe through this part, passing
    his feet sticking out from under the sheets.
    Stop! He's turning over.
    The mountain rearranges itself and crawls
    back into the dream, that deep mouth.

It's morning, he's off to work. His hands clean
    as a baby's.

Butcher's in the bank. His desk neat: each pad,
    pencil, loan request arranged geometrically
    like a Mondrian. Here come the customers!

Butcher checks the vault. Smells new money.

Butcher's at his desk. His foot held above the button
    on the floor. Sips his tea. Waits breathlessly
    for the gun-wielding, stocking-faced, blood-thirsty
    robber.

The First Of Everything

The first hand
does not touch you.
It is a warning.
There is the breath of rocks
a face that holds papers down.
And the first foot
does not step out.
It too is a warning.
You see it approach on a clear night,
its heel full of crushed berries.
A reminder, but of what?
The first eye has no need of seeing
and this too
in a way you cannot understand
is a warning.

These warnings slow you down.
Then, thumping your back door
like the morning paper
comes the first mouth
tied with string
and never mind what it says
you take it as a warning.

The first of everything
revolves like a planet
around your mind.
Your standing at the front door
is a warning.
So is your walking out.
Your day is a road
broken only by bridges.

Giving The Names To Poetry

Birds uphold and princes fart.
Along the world and around it
runs a silver ridge.

Donald Zelanka,
Jerry Pinero,
Martin Shapiro,
you'll never read your names in this poem.
Maybe one of you is a lawyer
but I doubt it.
Your names go with your faces,
your lives.
One of you still wears white socks, I bet
with brown shoes.
And who still jingles coins in his baggy slacks
(God, who wore "slacks" in 3rd grade?),
and one must work now
in his father's fruit stand on Carrolton Avenue.
I can just see you
Jerry Pinero
weighing a pound of peaches while you wonder
how your name got into poetry.
And that donkey laugh of yours,
Donald Zelanka,
do your kids own it now,
with that silver watch chain
half-mooned on your belt
(God, who wore watch chains in 3rd grade!), and
Martin,
Martin Shapiro,
I know you died of leukemia
three weeks before your bar mitzvah,
and I saw you in the coffin, too,

white, yeshiva face, and you still had dandruff.
What a big dope you were,
a big Jewish dope.
In a natural history museum
I'd figure to find you behind a glass labeled:
Rare Species—The Jewish Dope.

What is this
when the world gets suited up for winter
with slow moving skies
and the only sound I hear is the humming of the refrigerator
in the cold kitchen.
What is this that I think of you,
Donald Zelanka,
Jerry Pinero,
Martin Shapiro.
What is this that I wonder
what names like yours are doing now in the world,
names typed on credit statements,
traffic tickets,
letters from Shreveport.
What is this that makes me want
to give your names to poetry,
where a ridge is all there is
dividing birds from princes
and its world gives nothing away?

Mid Leap

I used to know what I was
talking about.

Now I know what I'm
talking about.

Inflection changes the meaning of what you are
talking about.

Re-read the second stanza and you'll see what I'm
talking about.

You could overhear, for instance, someone talking about
his lover but would you know what he was talking about
if you'd never had a lover.

Does the fish, showing off,
suffocate mid-leap?

Imagine two strangers embracing in an airport.

Talk about tacky.
Talk about science.

Assume the world strays and somehow never returns.
Do you say, "Here boy! Here boy!"
or do you wait and examine your fingernails.

Anarchy depends on perfect communication.
Its bright stare fools us.
But we love to be fooled.
Those of us with lovers are constantly fooled.
It's a way of showing off.
In a situation like this you can always
talk about

something else.

The Short Poem

The short poem
comes in
perfectly dressed
long metallic heels
that click
click   click
until seated
and hands on each knee
the short poem
bends forward
opening
like a spy
a small black bag
and removes
first one
then two at a time
seven white marbles
which are rolled
on the floor
to your feet.

When you pick these marbles up
all seven of them
first one
then the next six
in pairs
and bring them to your mouth,
suddenly,
looking across the room
you see
that the short poem
has somehow,
without so much as a *click,*

gone.

The Lost Things

I lost my hiking boots.
And my green sleeping bag.
Maybe someone stole them.
Anyway, they're gone.
So is my copy of
Hear Us O Lord
From Heaven
Thy Dwelling Place
by Malcolm Lowry.
So are some of my other books.
Daniele left my red baseball cap
with the silver wings of mercury
in the bathroom at Barbera's Pizza Parlor.
And I can't find my favorite pair of scissors
either, not to mention
my Bluit camping stove
and large cooking pot.
I loaned them to Karen Kaplowitz
coming out of the Cucamonga Wilderness
and she still has them.
She's a lawyer.
Now my mail isn't coming.
Someone put in a change of address form
and the post office
has been forwarding my mail
to the Graduate Department of English
at the University of Pittsburgh.
This is true.
"Why am I losing these things,"
I keep asking.
I keep asking this.
Out loud.
I'm driving Lori crazy.

"Something strange is going on here,"
I yell.
It's getting hard to concentrate on anything
for very long.
"Where are my boots," I whine
in the middle of a movie.
My favorite hiking boots.
It's very distressing.
Someone has my sleeping bag right now
and they're hurting it.
Someone's grimy hands are pulling apart
Hear Us O Lord From Heaven Thy Dwelling Place
and they don't even care about the underlines
or the notes I've made in the margins.
I'm not going to let it get me.
The red hat, with the silver wings of mercury,
I plan to get back if it's the last thing I do.
I'll keep a look out
and someday whoever took it
will be wearing it in the May Co.
thinking I've forgotten all about it.
But I haven't.
I'll see it.
And I'll get it back.
I'll get all my things back.
My Bluit camping stove
and my large cooking pot.
And my mail, all my mail.
My sleeping bag.
My boots.
My broken-in hiking boots.
I've missed you all so much.
So very much.
The lost things are coming back.
It's all coming back to me.
And I need to feel that I deserve this.
I need to learn

how to open my arms
and take them in,
as I would myself,
lost
these many
many
years.

Nearing The Point

Nearing the point
where the point at center
and once on its own
transforms earth to water
and back up above the shore line
around the unnecessary eyes
of its fish.
And each too to have seen it,
this black eagle
that flies out from your throat
and refuses to sing.
In our twentieth century
not because of me
not because of you
love is denied
kept silent
touches in departing
brushes us with wingtips
in cornerless space.
And higher still,
each out of desperation,
in orbit,
a little weaker,
reckless, sprung from the bedhead
where only yesterday
we stood
surrounded by the white ash
of our bodies.
So if not dead from the black water,
then dead from the frost,
from the window from the contrary idea
and so dead in fact from peace.
Convinced by the rooms we have loved in,

I get up from my chair
and walk toward the door
in this name flying up like a balloon,
while on the earth
there is time between points
to swim up from dreams
and smell your lover's shoulder
so deep in the earth's arms of sleep.

To Write A Poem

When I sit down to write a poem
I try not to think about anything.
Sometimes, I begin with a line
that just comes to me,
a line that might make no sense whatever,
and then I have to go on from there
making more lines that make no sense
until I've found a way before the end
to make it all make sense,
some kind of sense.
Now, I'm not known for being abstract,
so when Michael Ford asks me later
at The Lair where we all go for coffee
after the poetry workshop,
"Why are you writing so abstract?"
all I can answer is,
"That was abstract?"
I look down at the poem
and it doesn't seem abstract to me.
I read the beginning out loud.
"Nearing the point where the point
at center and once on its own
transforms earth to water and back
up above the shore line
around the unnecessary eyes
of its fish.— What's so abstract about that?"
I ask.
Michael tries an answer, but it's
abstract, too.
Bob says
I should cut the line
about my name flying up like a balloon.
And I agree with him.

Enough about my name.
My flying name.
Though, I think, the name too is abstract,
a rock I keep cracking into pieces,
or a balloon that does what balloons do,
and I wish it would make up its mind,
abstract flying cracking name.
Fist, rocket, staircase.
What's in an abstract flying name, anyway?
Did you know that *slug* spelled backwards is *guls.*
Think about that
if you want to understand what abstract means.
And I find also that I tend to leave the poems
I write
somewhere in the middle and then have to come back
to them somewhere before the end.
Like now. Like here, in this poem.
And just what the flying hell is a poem anyway?
Huh?
Huh?
HUH?
(pause)
I didn't think you knew.
Well if you don't know
how come you're always combing their hair
and holding your hands over their mouths
and tying their shoelaces together?
I see all the poems we've strapped
and tied to straight-backed chairs
in cold basement rooms,
barely bringing enough water
and bread to choke on.
I'd set them all free—
hordes of all our poems
descending upon us
in rage.
And my own head hurts.

And I'm sick of seeing my body
fill with the death of poetry.
I'm fat and getting fatter.
I can't stop eating.
I'm sick of poetry and sick of being fat.
I'm sick of combing my hair.
Sick of wearing the one shirt that fits me,
sick of seeing my desk piled with mail
and paper clips and unpaid bills,
sick of sleeping all day
and eating all night
and sick of praise and sick of grief
and sick of misunderstandings
and sick of love
and sick of fucking
and sick of jerking off
and sick of poetry, that's for sure,
sick of my poetry and sick of your poetry,
sick of everyone's poetry,
sick of reading
and sick of baseball
and sick of movies
and sick of the horses—
I like Charlie Chaplin
but I'm sick of just about everything else
and that includes poetry
which includes everything anyway.
And I'm sick of this poem, too.
This poem that makes such sense,
that flies off, like my name.
It nears the point
where the point at center
and once on its own
transforms earth to water
and back
up above the shoreline
around the unnecessary eyes

of its fish.
And it's abstract.

Like a rock.

Like a slug
that
spelled backwards
becomes a large white bird
that screams out in the air
and flies far
far away.

The Lover

A book with a picture on the cover
of a lady dressed in red on my desk.
This woman I love
tying her tennis shoes up on her feet.
A root-briar pipe,
straight-grained and carbon-caked
leaning on the rim
of the cork-centered ash tray.
A memory in the room
that settles like netting
as I enter,
the big house with winding
tunneled stairs.
These I own, these thoughts,
that book,
the woman I love,
my pot-bowled pipe.
And they own me,
they stretch and spread
and suck my flesh
not just into themselves
but out to air,
out above the hills and water,
in touch with
some un-named holy voice
that calls me to my life.
And I am this one man
attached beyond beauty
to forms I cannot imitate.
And woman too,
I touch my nipples
and run my hands over the cool
flesh of my ass,

and I am woman too,
barely sensing that other beauty
I lost long ago.
And I touch each part of me
that walks in red dresses,
that thing smoked
those shoes laced,
these memories loved.
And I am open,
if not always,
then now,
to leave my hands on table-tops
and give up,
to let go,
to walk from my bed
in the morning,
open a window,
lean out,
open my mouth to speak,
say nothing but song,
to flap my arms
and fly off,
to sail out
beyond the map
of my own
un-
traveled face.

Bodies

At first I am talking
about my body,
then something else.
What do you know
about bodies.
When Ben and I
have to move them
from one table to another
they're so heavy
and stubborn and clumsy.
Ben lifts the head
and puts a block underneath.
It's like lifting a broken desk lamp.
I swing the feet up
and straighten them.
Always under the cover.
When I go home
I sometimes think about
the part of my own body
I am soaping in the shower.
This hand holding *this* breast.
Why does touching myself here
feel better than touching myself
there?
Whose hands would feel better?
There is so much about bodies
I don't understand.
Sometimes, after we make love,
I discover that I'm bleeding.
There's a spot on the sheets,
and between my legs when I wipe myself
in the bathroom.
He comes in to watch, concerned.
Blood comes off in my hands

but after a bit the bleeding stops.
We're both naked.
There's a little blood on his penis.
I watch him wash it in the sink.
It's as if he were bleeding too.
Back in bed, lying side by side,
we talk about the bodies
then fall asleep.
When I wake during the night
I can hear his heavy breathing.
I lay my hand across his belly.
He turns and snugs his ass
up against my side
and I turn with him
throughout the night;
a kind of dance, a breathing,
a small exchange of words.
To wake in the morning
beside someone you love
is a miracle in itself.
Then the bodies get up
and have breakfast.

There is no insurmountable solitude.
All paths lead to the same goal:
To convey to others what we are.

Pablo Neruda
Toward The Splendid City
Nobel Lecture

Another Sentence

Every sentence is another sentence,
really another life.
Someone's always one step ahead.
The streets glow from the snow plow's blade
chipping up stone with a daylight flash.
From here, the same tree out back,
the same asphalt roof,
the same wounded clothespins
shifting on the line.
Sometimes the man hanged is a hero,
sometimes a traitor.
Perfect sight and perfect blindness
when it suits our needs.
One day you realize
that you cannot break out
of your own bones.
There is snow-mush in the gutters
and along the edge of the highway,
melting here, turning to rock there.
Something's always a step ahead.
Every sentence is another life,
really another sentence.

The Surrealist Poem

Just a minute.
Can't you see I'm talking to someone.
Come back another time.
Or wait until I'm finished.
See that goldfish over there,
The one with the mag wheels
And carnation in its lapel
Right next to my copy of *New Directions*.
You can't miss it.
Where is your heart.
Why are you so sad.
Live a little.
There's still time.
You can't lose.

A Burning

Old cans full of sour milk
stacked in the back room,
his shoes, boxes of them,
not to throw anything away,
even shoelaces for sentiment
remembered in leaning cardboard boxes
once used to pack pillows before
the house burned down.
He smells that all the time:
the dry burning wood,
wet strips of ash and black puddles of water.
Sometimes he can trace the smell to something real.
Sometimes, to something else, coming or having come.
It will come again, he reasons,
and begins again to pack things away
so that what will burn will burn together,
each head in its proper place.

I remember his standing out back without tie or hat
looking up at the house, his shoes caked with mud
and the black marbles of charcoal he kicks with his toes.
The palmetto trees take up the sounds of the wind
and pass them down Elysian Fields Avenue.
A storm is coming
and I catch the bristle run up my back
as I watch him from the window
stoop to the burned pieces of wood,
the half-blackened fence posts,
a piece of metal covered with ash.
He stands and turns and sees me,
and I rise the man above him to him the boy below me
afraid to look at the unburned skin of his own hands.
Later, he brings the smell in with him to the table,

and leaves it on the chairs, and the sofa,
and the bed he takes for a month.
The last day with us he spends
talking to my father in the kitchen,
his hands flopped like fish in his lap,
and the burning and the burned
spread across the life of his back.
Had my father lived I might have yet remembered to ask
just who he was in his black coat,
this man with bad breath who looked at me in fright
as some other life unburned.
Had my father lived,
I might have yet asked just who he was:
A half-brother?
A friend? Another
Jew, passing through.
But I am not ungrateful of puzzles that grow strong
against the known and the sure,
nor the smell a man brings and takes with him.
I have that smell too somewhere.
I can recognize it from blocks away,
and sometimes days ahead.
I can look at you and tell if the smell of a burning in me
is the same as the smell of a burning in you.
I can tell who brings it in their hands,
how the bleach of their faces
wants one such burning to replace another.

Some Life

Some life that seems better than none
and all the beautiful women
who do their hair with Head shampoo
and never spill the ketchup.

inside the nightingale
the bat
and inside the leopard
the leopard

Now there are women
who sit with other women
or they sit alone
and I sit alone and watch them.
Just once I'd like one to get up
and come over to my table
and ask to sit and talk.
Give me that chance to show
that I am a man
who would make friends with women
and just that
and no more,
as if that were an honorable
place to stop,
an easy place to come to.

Some life is always better than none.
Inside each of us
that other animal,
as proud as hungry as fearful
as dangerous.

I think women are afraid of us

because we murder in ourselves
what they love too much in life to lose,
and there is no room now for love,
or friendship.

But I am not afraid of you.
I love your smells,
I love the blood that stains your underwear.
I love the rash under your arms
and the fat
below your buttocks & between your thighs
you pinch and wish away.
And that illusion of self
we both adhere to,
well...
we can forgive each other
for wanting this darkness
to see itself first in the eyes of the enemy.

Some life is all we have.
A marriage that lasts 10 years;
A love affair for 2;
A weekend with a stranger;
A voice on the phone—
wrong number.

and inside the nightingale
the bat
and inside the leopard
the leopard

Some men; some women;
some life.

Each one
inside
the other.

Poem Without Picture
for Picture Without Poem

Dear *American Poetry Review*:
Enclosed are several pictures of me,
one of which
I would like you to consider
for publication in your paper.
I realize that along with each
poet's picture
you print a poem or two,
but I'm not sure I have any
that you would like.
Can I have a picture
without a poem
published?
I feel so different
with the camera.
The poem, of course,
is another matter.
I could just as well
fall flat on the page
and be done with it—
this creeping out
word by word
takes my breath away.
The pictures, though,
remain whole.
You can see where I gained weight
last summer
and the beard I grew
for a lover.
But smiling or not,
they're all just me,

arms open,
placing all that dumb trust
in this dumb world.
Sometimes, just looking at those pictures,
I want them to change me,
to give me back
the face I've been.
But, it's still my face
looking back at all of you,
daring you all to look back.
I've been looking back
at all the poets' pictures
you've published since you began.
They're good faces.
We've got such strong, healthy,
beautiful poets in this country.
It's time to face the poem
of all our faces,
and it's good that there's a place
we can look back at each other.
Thanks for considering *my* face.
Sincerely yours,

    Jack Grapes

Trying To Get Your Life In Shape

It's like doing the roof.
Just when you've got the slate set,
the tacks in your mouth,
the tar hot and ready,
your foot accidentally
nudges the hammer
and it begins to slide away
from you
like a christened ship.
Down it goes.
You hear the crash below,
take a deep breath, say *shit*,
and turn for the ladder
just as it
catches a wind
and begins the long lean
away from your outstretched hand.
Aw shit!
You look up.
Storm clouds from out of nowhere
belly over the setting sun.
The dark ice age is at hand.
And no one is home.
And the doors are locked.
Your baloney sandwich
has been pecked away by birds.
You sit back,
you contemplate this new richness
come into your life,
and shiver on the roof
knowing it could be worse.
Why you could be inside.
Warm by the fire.

Sipping sherry.
Shoes off.
Just
temporarily
alive.

End Of Conversation
Overheard On A Train

"...and so
his foot
was of no further
use to him...

not as a foot
that is."

My Life

Now that's a log cabin if I ever saw one!
Someone else left that message.
I'm fishing.

Yet another silver fender blade.
See around the edges all those paper cuts.
But with summer this close, ear to jaw.
Lovers just don't care for politics.

You can wear any coat to the dance.
If all black then you must know something.
Each vest should contain a secret.
Who did you kill wearing those shoes?

I have this delicate relationship with dreams.
Run for your life!
Will this gray rain ever stop!
The closer I look, the less I dream.

Some say there's method to one's madness.
Delirium is robbed of its meager truth
as madness if it's called a *Work of Art*.
The chance to see being born, over and over.

After awhile, even deSade bores me.
Violence promises to recover the self,
but you can't limit the world that wounds you
any more than you can disappear into Nature
when Nature is invisible to begin with.

To lose everything at the movies
is an act of faith.
Scene. Close-up. Tracking shot. Dissolve.
You think that's something.
You should see my life.

What Is Wrong With The Weather

points of stars
small crabbed webs
if anything can gleam
a fall
hair brush
on my sister's
another morning
lap
and pencil
barely audible
testing memory
so much wrong
with the weather
he is inside
thinking
the time to get it right
is now
both hands
around both hands
look up
the stars
unable to breathe
till you do.

Why I Am Not A Sardine

After Frank O'Hara

I'm not a sardine, I'm a painting.
Why? I guess I'd rather be a
sardine, but I'm not. Well,

for example, Michael Ford
is cutting a poem into shreds. I drop in.
"Hang out the window and bleed," he
says. I hang; we bleed. I look
up. "You've got some poem there."
"Yes, it needs shredding THIS POEM."
"Oh," I go and the years fly by
and I'm still bleeding. I stop by.
The poem is still being shredded
into smaller and smaller pieces.
And the years go by, bleeding,
the two of us, almost finished.
"The poem's finished," he says.
"Where's the poem?"
All that's left is blood.
"It was too much," Mike says.

But me? One day I am eating a sardine.
A silver sardine. I bleed into its mouth.
Pretty soon it's a whole fish of blood,
not even a fish anymore, shredded.
Then another shred, scale upon scale.
Lifesize to scale.
Wonderful silver. Bloodthirsty.
There are more fish than sardines.
Life is horrible. Fish accept
the passage of time; the days

go by; years shredded into poets.
My meal is finished and I haven't even
mentioned I've been hanging out the window
all this time.
And one day, at a poetry reading,
Mike throws confetti over his audience,
and announces that it's not a poem,
but his old friend, Jack, a sardine.

The Serious Poem

There is no time.

And you can't win.

Confessional

I wish I could write it once and easy
to belong to me.
It always belongs to you.
And you never care to know
if it's once and easy
when it's yours.
What is going to grow in the heart
that is not ventured
or given with the hands open and up
to being within you again
when all you can say is how saddled horses
wait by the tent
or how mountains predict misfortune
or how your legs are the legs of a woman
and your breasts too yet you are afraid
of what you really know, believe only
what they tell you.
Everything you dare not say
truly yours
and so abandoned, like a viewpoint.
Will you count insults and grievances
or stand once and easy with the grief.
I wish I could write it once
and it would belong to me
and no one else,
but it always belongs to you.

To My Father, The Captain

In this wake
where blood separates me from midwives,
my father lies in his coffin,
engines cut,
his face done up,
still commanding me
not to exceed him.

But what excess, and whose?
I can go too far, I can not go
far enough.
Either way you win.
Dad, all I know in this life
is the way
through excess:
Too much pie in the face;
Too much flesh on the bone;
Too many words.

Power in the perfect ending,
In the gold piece
on the dining room table
Power to make your son
frozen in his life
the way you were
in yours.

You never thought
the gift of poetry
you gave like a meager token
would set me free.
I do this for myself, Dad,
not for you.

For you, I would
peel my flesh away,
inhabit stale bedrooms;
For you,
I would never try hard enough,
sell shoes,
look for my face
on the bathroom floor
where you told me it would be.
But look at the dream I am rising from.
For you,
I would chisel the stone
in my chest,
walk with my shoulders bent forward,
mumble my name.
For you, I would ride the whale down
to your ship on the reef,
not shine for myself
in his belly.

For me
I write this poem.
This is the power Daddy:
That I will finish this poem
the way I want to,
with my name,
not the way you'd have liked,
with yours.

love,
    Jack

On Raising The Hand

On Tuesdays I get up at 4:30 A.M.
to teach poetry in the schools.
My first class starts at 7:20—
it's called *zero period,*
which to me is very ominous
as if it were the final meeting
before the end of the world,
a final poetic countdown.
The students are tired, you can tell,
and drag on in without saying much—
to me— to each other.
When I read a poem and ask who liked it,
no one raises a hand.
"So how many didn't like the poem?" I ask.
Still, no one says a thing; no hands go up.
This is zero period. Barely out of sleep.
We sit drugged like flies at the screen.
I go home tired as well, feeling I've failed.
It's best to think of this as just a job.
I get paid for this, and that makes me honorable.
Poetry doesn't. Poetry gets me vacant stares.
And yet, from this thing we pay so little for,
we want so very much.
Sleepy, tired, educationally bewildered,
what they want is for me to set something on fire,
to open a door to another world,
to change them.
For a penny I'd throw myself at their feet
just as long as they'd embrace this thing
that sucks the blood from me and speaks always
in more voices than I can hear at one time
while the monotonous voice of the world drones on
about how to keep from dying in the cold of a strange city.

And then, today I come home and read the poems
they have written after weeks of treading
the waters of process.
Richard writes:
    "Was it you who used to look
    people in the eye?"
David writes:
    "This is not all that matters I like this.
    Life it is not out this class."
Cindy feels she's being tortured and starved,
    "maybe for being beautiful, instead of useful."
Sam thinks
    "writing
    is the first of all things...
    that builds up the world."
Charlie looks into the fishbowl and wonders if there is
    "loneliness in the unblinking eyes" of his guppy.
Bobby writes that
    "Dancing shoes that dive with desire
    tremble with the fear they've failed."
And Tom ends his poem:
    "The glory that cloaks me is dying."

I read their poems in the early morning and raise my hand.
They've set something on fire.
They've opened a door for me.
I embrace their words, their courage.
In the cold of a strange city,
I keep from dying,
both my hands go up.

No Way To Break A Branch

This is no way to break
a branch.

The eels would not fear
you.

Imagine it is your neck.
Suck up your courage.
The juice of life calls.

Forget technique.
Go to it.   Dig in.

To Board The Bus

Just make enough sense
to board the bus,
he said.
I board the bus
but I don't make sense,
I said.
Better to make sense,
he said, and stand in the street.
I stand in the street
but get nowhere for all my sense, I said.
For all your sense,
he said,
You don't have to go anywhere.
People will come to you.
They will board the bus?
I asked.
Exactly, he said.
Then let's stand
and make sense together,
I said.
Two of us making sense,
he said,
and the world will move.
Exactly, I said. I feel it already.
What you feel, he said
is the bus coming our way.
Then let it pass, I said.

The Children Look For Crabs
On The Beach

There's a reason for this:
You put on your trunks and go stand by the water, watch
the guts of this planet wash up on the sand.
Two girls dig in the root-bones of a plastic-looking sea plant.
They say they are looking for crabs for their collection
and show you a half-filled paper cup stuck in the wet sand.
I'm not satisfied not knowing anymore
what is wrong with me,
what storm is tearing me apart
plank by plank on the rough sea.
I'm not satisfied anymore going from metaphor to metaphor:
a sinking ship,
a drowning sailor,
a beached hulk of a sea monster blinded on the beach
being picked apart by children.
I look out to sea and read the poets for comfort,
but if poetry is to save me,
it'll have to be my own, full of lies and mischief,
and the one paperweight of truth
that keeps everything from flying off.
I want to toss that paperweight out to sea,
that smug stone so breathless on my desk.
So I go back to my car,
shake the sand out of my shoes,
check the mirror to see if I've gotten any sun.
What do I need sun for anyway?
What do I need anything for anyway?
Why can't I fix the sink?
Why am I not more ambitious?
Why won't I come back to me?
I drive off down the highway

in my car that needs fixing everywhere.
God, I feel like a housewife
in someone else's soap opera.
Christ, I feel like laughing.

Orestes

Remember the truth
is all that changes.
Lies remain the same,
true to their cracks.
One degree at a time.
Oblivious to the mark.
Certainty is the lie
that lures us
once and for all
to be once and for all
true.
Made perfect by suffering.

Final Exam

Can you have a spree of cheese?

Would you loan a bank a flush?

Why is the back door of your house
    so morbid?

When you tie your shoes, do you
    indicate with word or gesture
    your preference for boots
    or do you have something
    to hide?

Say three words that don't dissolve
    or melt or evaporate or turn
    to powder and blow away
    without a fare-thee-well or
    so much as a kiss.

Dillinger puts a nickel on the porch
    when he wants a newspaper
    but now he's dead. Some say
    he's alive still. Is this fair
    and why must the law
    protect the innocent?

Are you tired, listless, depressed, suicidal,
    rabid, loquacious, engaged, visionary,
    plastic, fiber, traffic, a kosher
    pickle, exact change? How could you
    stop this and change your life?

Would you rather live in New York or

cash a ten dollar bill?

What does the word *gaberlunzie* mean?
  Look it up.

Why is symmetry happy? How does grief expand?
  Is retribution a crystal?

Think of someone you've offended, grieviously
    wronged. Is there any way you could
    make it worse? Is there any area that
    remains unwounded? What are the prospects
    for permanent injury? Is your day booked,
    or do you have time to settle this matter?

How do you adjust?

Why does the broom whisk; is there an edge
    to an elephant; what mystery burns your heart
    the best?

Home Free

We're buying groceries for dinner
so I plunk two quarters into the slot machine
stationed by the check-out counter
and on the second quarter hit a $12 jackpot.
The tin cup is designed to make it seem like I've blown up
Fort Knox and bells go off to let the customers know
there's a silver waterfall, one to a customer.
I'm hooked and I know it.
I give the money away, three bucks apiece to Vern
and Katharine and Lori, saying here's some lucky quarters
but I'm really just trying not to hoard the luck.
Too much might go off in my hands.
Too much might alert the gods.
This luck is stolen, and after all the other luck
that's come my way—well, I've got to be careful
is all. Now we're in the casino,
the big time. Vern hits a $50 jackpot.
I'm at the blackjack table losing my breath.
Lori and Katharine are in the bar picking up strangers
while UCLA loses on a field goal to Arizona.
I lose another $20 at blackjack waiting for my free drink.
By the time we leave I'm $60 down, probaly $100.
Next day at the Crystal Bay Club I pick up $100
at blackjack. Lori convinces me to leave a winner.
But I know I'll be back. The next morning we're back
and I drop $120. By the time we get to Reno
I can't tell for sure if I'm up or down.
Quarters go into the machines as I go by.
I'm pulling handles down the way I'd strip bark
from a tree or rickety-rick a stick against a fence
when I was a kid. I walk by a blackjack table, bet $40
and win. Walk off and put chips on roulette and lose.
Fork up a few bills at another table and win on two kings.

Bells go off, lights blink.
All you have to do here is win one jackpot,
one big fat fucking jackpot and the rest is history.
Lori's grabbing my arm and Katharine's hungry
and Vern's walking slow and easy out the door.
This quarter, this next quarter, this $5 yellow chip.
this $25 black chip, this is the one that does it,
one more plunk one more pull of the handle and it's done,
we're home free, we escape the pull of gravity,
we're off this rotten earth and heading for the stars.
"Lose here, win everywhere else," I say
as we get back in the car.
Merry Christmas, friends. Happy New Year.

I Just Had To Tell You

Listen I just had to tell you
I wrote five poems today.

Can you believe it
five poems.

Russia's still in Afghanistan
the hostages are still hostages
ah forget 'em
another storm coming
and another one for Sunday
fuck it
radioactive rain
the candidates on TV
elect 'em all for all I care
we need ten presidents anyway
all those homes slipping into mud

destruction

death

one man looking for his wife
another girlfriend
hoping her lover is alive
and they're starving in Asia
and the blacks in Africa
are overrunning the white man's cities
well, come on
drop the bombs here for a change
swarm up our black beaches
set fire to the whole Archipelago—
taxi A-bomb sewer rats parades

the tired and the hungry and the weak
up from the bottom of the sea
the molten core of the earth
and comets strike us, asteroids
planets off their course
another sun moving our way
fuck it fuckit fckit
I wrote five poems today.

This is the sixth.
Whoooopeeeeeee!

So Many

So many plays
and novels
and stories
and essays
and history books
and philosophy
and science fiction
and fiction
and science.
I thought once I was going to write them,
a novel, or a story, or a play.
I don't think so anymore.
It's so hard to write a novel.
You have to work at it every day
and you have to type up at least 200 pages,
even if you never go to a second draft.
And a play?
All those characters,
and scenes, and lights,
the changing sets,
and worst of all
the actors, acting.
Genghis Khan, Attila, Hitler,
Vlad the Impaler
are nothing compared to what
actors can do to a play
once they get to say the words out loud.
No, I won't be writing any plays.

And stories, fiction...
what can I say.
Men left the tribe and headed into the dark forest,
climbed out over the black mountains

and were gone for years. We were children
when they left,
but when our children mark off
a new boundary with boulders,
they come back, full of scars, jewels,
and strange women with shaved heads.
And they begin to tell stories.
And our children listen, and we listen,
and the weather and the seasons
and the sun on its way across
stop until the stories are all told.
That's what I think about
when I think about stories.
I won't be writing
any of those.

What, that's not in a play, or a novel,
or a story
can I possibly tell you.
How can I write enough and the kind of words
that conceal the lack
of anything true.

There is only this one,
true, utterly beautiful poem.
And each of us, possibly one time
in our lives,
can write it.
I would like to do that.
I would like to try that.
And when you write yours
I would like to hear it.
It's the same poem, each of us have to write.
So we'll know it when we see it.
So many plays, and novels, and stories.
But only one
poem.

I Like My Own Poems

I like my own poems
best.
I quote from them
from time to time
saying, "A poet once said,"
and then follow up
with a line or two
from one of my *own* poems
appropriate to the event.
How those lines sing!
All that wisdom and beauty!
Why it tickles my ass
off its spine.
"Why those lines are mine!"
I say
and Jesus, what a bang
I get out of it.

I like the *ideas* in them,
my poems,
ideas that hit home.
They *speak* to me.
I mean, I understand
what the hell
the damn poet's
talking about.
"Why I've been there,
the same thing," I shout,
and Christ! What a shot it is,
a shot.

And hey.
The words.

Whew!
I can hardly stand it.
Words sure do not fail
this guy, I say.
From some world
only he knows
he bangs the bong,
but I can feel it
in the wood,
in the wood of the word,
rising to its form
in the world.
"Now, you gotta be good
to do that!" I say
and damn! It just shakes
my heart,
you know?

"Shall we put in the heart now?"

Dr. Ernst Praetorius
The Bride Of Frankenstein

The Poet's Funeral

Friends, we write the eulogy
and it is crap.
We praise the bird that barely
survives the rainstorm,
we make miracles of the poetry
written on, what?—paper!
and not the other kind
that is just her arms around me.
We believe the spirit
does not die with the man
when most often it dies before.
Shovel the bastard down, I say
and cover the pine with leaves.
A kick of dust and a what's for supper
will do any time.
Flesh!
Even now you're more concerned
with your itching leg
that sets the table and warms the palm
just midnight to a lover
and as it should be!
Talk to me for chrissakes! is what I say.
Toss the glass once in the air
and let it smash wine and all and say
good for that and riddance.
Stalk your own hearts and be ruthless about it,
swing each high in the air and wait
for the music to begin again
and when it does
with a hard hard heel and laughter
that fills a fist,
dance on, dance on.

Here's A Poem

Here's a poem that has not
been revised or rewritten
or read aloud or cut
or extended or given to a lover.
Here's a poem that
has no code word, no
name for something else,
no intended meaning,
no ax to grind.
Here's a poem inconsequential
as a thumbtack.
Give me a penny for it
and you've overpaid.
Lose it and it's still there
for all that it was worth.
Here's a poem less than
twenty lines.
Defend it.

Voyage

Now on the table
all my friends in ties
waving goodbye.
This voyage.
And so much time
taken to learn again
what we once knew
from each other
and forgot.
It's still daylight
but I can see the moon.
Almost
or so it seems
transparent.
Not even a full moon.
But a full moon.

Passing The Ketchup

She says pass the ketchup
and I grab the salt shaker
and stretch it across the table.
"The ketchup," she says.

The lawn chair's full of rust
and the nylon straps in straggles.
It leans in the corner of the garage.
"Let's throw it out," she says.
"Not yet," I tell her. "Maybe we'll find
something to do with it."

We come home from the beach
and a trail of ants
flow to and from
the sugar bowl
down the counter to the floor
and out the screen door.
"Look at them all!" she shouts.
So I do.

These men grow old in my body.
They take such slow steps,
and take all morning
to drink a glass of milk.
They find nothing familiar
in the familiar,
debate the eye of the city
and the hand of the country.
They fall asleep in the kitchen.

"Where are the car keys?" she asks.
"The car keys," I repeat,

unable to remember
what is a car
and what is a key.
Finally:
"In the car," I say.
"The keys."

I wake in the middle of the night
to answer the phone.
Hello. Hello.
Nothing but the sound of someone's breathing
coming from the other end.
It sounds like my own,
but I can't be sure.
"Who was it?"
"Who was what?"
"On the phone!"
"Me. I think."

Today I sit on the beach
and watch the waves come in,
break in a stiff white line
forty feet out,
and carry the boogie-boarders
to the edge of the sand still standing.
There is nothing on the horizon.
Not a storm coming our way,
not a black ship,
no land.
We are all stretched on beach towels
inching the white breast out for a tan.
We are all lying here at the edge
of a continent.

I get up and brush the sand from my body.
I take the napkins we brought
with the food in the ice-chest

and stick one each into my ears
and nose: wings of a sort.
Then another I roll for a fang.
Insert it under my top lip,
hunch over, and limp down the sand
like a walrus trying to dance
on the edge of the berm.
The kids step back at first,
then begin to mimick me;
finally, they join in, following me
as our footprints just above the water line
one on top of the other
change and grow larger, deeper.
A single new life form
come out of the water,
come out from the land.

"What do you think you're doing?" she calls.

"Passing the ketchup," I say.

A Deed Of Light

My sister dies.
I am not born yet.
She barely strikes soul
and goes.
My Uncle Jack dies.
I am not born yet.
It is right
to give me his name.
Among other things
it means
something smaller
than the usual of its
kind;
a small stuffed puppet
set up to be pelted
for sport.
For years they call me
Jackie.
My father sneers.
What kind of name is that!
Uncle Charles dies.
Everyone in the kitchen
stands and cries.
A year later
on the kitchen floor
Uncle Lou dies
vomiting on the newspaper
under his head.
I bring him more newspaper.
My socks flap at the toes.
My name is Jack:
a small national flag
flown by a ship.

The next year
we move to the new house.
This time of brick.
Martin Shapiro dies.
My mother drags me to the wake.
In the open coffin
his face
can be seen
all the way from the back
of the chapel.
Applejack, jacknife,
jack-o-lantern.
Aunt Adela dies
all summer in the back bedroom.
Withers on the sheets of cancer.
Jackie, she says,
show me the movies.
My mother prances
with grief around the grave.
Sarah Bernhardt.
A year later, of cancer too,
she gets it down.
Hisses bitch at the nurse
the last two days.
When I leave for Europe
I forget to tell my father
goodbye.
In Italy the phone rings.
Come home, it says,
you're the man in the family
now.
Jacksnipe, jackstraw,
jack-in-the-box.
From tides to bushes
on Sundays,
each of us digs holes
in the backyard.

This growing further apart.
Karl who is my brother.
Louis who is my brother.
Charlaine who is my sister.
Jacksmelt, jackshaft,
jackpot.
I am Daniele's Uncle Jack.
I am Benjamin's Uncle Jack.
I am Ari's Uncle Jack.
My arms become trees
solitary with the base pale face
of a green kitchen door,
jewels for teeth to kill my father,
see me, see you,
see who dies on Tuesday.

No more of graves and names.
On the dead I spit on the dead of the dead.
The Jack deads and the Charles deads
and the mother deads and the father deads.
My name beats the bush
that sends up flocks of birds.
This lantern cut to look
like a human face.
The name looks out of my eyes.
The meaning looks out of my name.
Jack is a deed of light.

Another Sleepwalk

So severe and desperate is the heart's resistance
to cold crying sleep
that its one finger thrusts up screaming
at particles of separation
the dead cough up.
No, it says. No.
Those gods who walk on thin legs
and refuse to speak
counsel us to do the same.
A speechless bravery.
Well, tracks beaten in the canefields
are more determined in their course
than we with our nail of science
on the one hand,
a brief and perfect faith on the other.

I do not always sleep in peace.
She wakes beside me and pads off into the kitchen,
and I know how large out there is darkness,
a plain brown pillow thrown to the corner
of the room.
It is there for her, beastly in its fold of gray,
loving another deep death deep deep within her
and I am afraid that one can swallow the other
as easily as I fall asleep again,
passing so easily into dream.

What a lovely and beautiful and tingling thing
this fear is
and I see my arms go out and take it all around.
And my fear in the night takes hold of itself
and dances back with the darkness.

How love can know from its losing
is beyond me,
but it does.
Yet the space grows to include us all.
We are big
for being so small
as to make the rest so large.

And we bring the light again
and say the words
and give the voice a shape
that says yes,
and again says yes.

Then:
lightswitch; footsteps; bedcover.

Then it is that her body slides up to mine
and the world
in its limping way
goes on.

Testimony

Why should I lie?
Ask any bed, the stutter gives it away.
One machine measures the heart beat;
others, more sophisticated,
the dilation of the eye,
the contraction of the pupil.
I still don't have a son
or for that matter, a daughter,
but loved as I am by children,
I wonder if I've not gone on already
in some larger way beyond paternity,
the excessive transformation of my genes.
I am still here, and still there,
and already continuing in concrete and ash.
Why should I even think of lying?
The real killers are to be congratulated,
slapped on the back and toasted
for their inscrutable ingenuity,
the way a decision is sounded like an earthquake.
I'm always appalled by the ones
who pucker their lips and cannot laugh.
The pain,
to be humourless, tightly bound by logic,
the very idea that understanding
is not a killing, knowledge not a form
of asphixiation.
It touches me that we whittle our lives down
to the smallest of entries in a notebook,
the notebook we carry with us on daily routine,
the notebook no one is ever allowed to read,
filled with one lie after another,
but our true children nonetheless.
Dare I let them out to have lives of their own?

Dare I give them up and admit
I am the father, I am the mother?
I would have my children carry on
with their own names, look back at me
and remember that what I did I did
out of love, that murder is always
an intentional accident, living easily
between the grain of expansion and the grain of collapse.
This is only part of the evidence.
I've never meant to lie.

Vows

We're going to get married
and have kids
and live together
and be bloody

Trees, Coffee,
And The Eyes Of Deer

Do you want coffee?
He was only nineteen when his first book of poems
    was published.
I wasn't going to go back.
I was going to sleep at the edge of the driveway
    in my sleeping bag,
      until all the cars
      went up in smoke and teach 'em.
My mother sat on the flesh of her face
      such grimness in her palms
      such unpitying bitterness.
But I digress.

The cities too in my back bedroom,
    18th Century St. Petersburg under the desk
      where it belongs;
    the Paris of Abelard and Eloise high
      on the carpet;
    smoky London and shrill New York take up
      the whole closet,
      and even tho I keep promising
      to farm the clutter,
      I just close my eyes
      when I reach for a shirt
      and slam the door shut again.

More coffee?
Sometimes inventing conversation is impossible.
      "Shall we get in the car?"
      "Your perfume smells lovely."
And everything is about three weeks, if it's important;

two months if a hand-me-down;
        a year if you like jazz or Isak Dinesen.
Then my father falls to the floor like a tree under
        thunder boom on his back and down comes
        the phone and the phone book boom and
        his startled eyes boom back at me
        because I had pushed him.
Lately I can't remember the dreams.
        When I wake, they scamper off, like deer.
        At best, I remember the eyes of the ones
        who stop and turn to look back at me.
        "I mean you no harm," I call out to them,
        but they swing and leap away.

The tree I can see from here next to the garage
        is still as a brick, and as smug.
        So solid to have lived this long,
        another life in the city worthier than mine,
        thick-barked to my own thin skin.
        "Fuck you, tree! Up yours!" I yell out the window.
But I digress.

No I don't. Nothing here is digression.
        If you can't tell digression from inclusion,
        why don't you try Hy's Deli on Beverly.
        They make a great brisket sandwich.
And in March, the deer from their winter of hunger
        come after the running dogs to be fed
        in the kitchen where my mother flips through
        the pages of my first book of poems.
        They mean nothing to her. Which is okay.
        It's the idea of them she can't stand.
        She holds the book the way you'd hold a rock
        that has just come flying through the window
        and landed messageless on the table.
        No one seems to know
        when my father is coming home.

"He may never come home," my sister says.
Mom pushes the book across the table
as though she were brushing aside a fly
that had landed on her arm.
"Up yours, too!" I say to her now,
dead tho she is.

Is this how people talk in a Russian novel?

Well I don't care anymore how they talk,
      how the dead persist in their life after death.
      It is us they need, not the other way around.
Today I take care of that tree, that goddamn tree.
      I'm going down there and pick a fight
      if I have to.
      Take it apart with my bare hands
      if it comes to that.

This is between us, the living.

*"Any landing
you can walk away from
is a good landing."*

Superchicken

Jack Grapes is a poet, playwright, actor, teacher, and the editor of *ONTHEBUS*, a literary journal. He has won several fellowships and grants in literature from the National Endowment for the Arts, and nine Artist-in-Residence grants from the California Arts Council. Author of 8 1/2 books of poetry, he also wrote and starred in *Circle of Will*, a comdy about the lost years of Will Shakespeare which ran for two years in Los Angeles and won two theatre critics awards for Best Comedy and Best Performance. As a Poet-in-Residence, he has worked in dozens of schools throughout the Los Angeles area as part of the California Poets-in-the Schools program, and teaches several private writing workshops as well. A native of New Orleans, he now lives in Los Angeles with his wife Lori and three-year-old son Josh.